# Retail Fashion Arithmetic

Charles Nesbitt

2

Copyright and ISBN page

**Also by Charles Nesbitt**

FUNDAMENTALS FOR SUCCESSFUL AND SUSTAINABLE FASHION BUYING AND MERCHANDISING

*

FUNDAMENTALS FOR FASHION RETAIL  STRATEGY PLANNING AND IMPLEMENTATION

*

FUNDAMENTALS FOR FASHION RETAIL ARITHMETIC, ASSORTMENT PLANNING AND TRADING

*

FUNDAMENTALS OF FASHION RETAIL, TECHNOLOGY, MANUFACTURING AND SUPPLIER MANAGEMENT

*

THE COMPLETE JOURNAL OF FASHION RETAIL BUYING AND MERCHANDISING

*

RETAIL FASHION PROCUREMENT TEAM ROLES AND PROCESSES

# Table of Contents

## PREFACE

The process of buying and selling in some form or other of goods has been with us since time immemorial. Often when one stands in bewilderment in an elegant shopping mall and wonder how all the stores are able to effectively seduce the many shoppers trawling the wide corridors to readily part with their well-earned money while at the same time enabling them to possibly enjoy a wonderful social experience.

The plan of offering goods to the potential customer is a complicated one and is a science that involves many players whose individual contributions slot seamlessly together and are so perfectly coordinated that it provides the perception that it is the result of one individual concerted effort.

It will be illustrated as to how the relationships of the major functions that intertwine from the conceptualisation of a product through to the presentation of a finished garment to the potential customer and in doing this demonstrates how the key areas such as buying, merchandising, technology, production, design, logistics and selling each with their unique specialised operations manage to achieve this.

The book endeavours to try and outline the basic key principles and mechanisms by which this happens and should be helpful to students, people in retailing and those who are maybe considering a career in the industry. For those who already are part of the fashion buying and merchandising community this book will be beneficial in that it provides a complete simplified overview of all the integral activities and roles that go to make up the topic and thereby will provide a broader insight into their own career.

The material of the book, other than that specifically referenced is the result of the author's own exposure to the subject during a career spanning thirty five years at a major retail organisation in Southern Africa, the support from colleagues, mentors, interaction with suppliers and own research. There has been some cross referencing to other books or technical material but the book focuses largely at a higher level on the key principles, concepts and theories and hence there is none or very little mention of retailers by name or technological packages for some key activities such as planning, allocating, critical path management, logistics and the like.

The fundamental purpose is therefore to provide the basic background that goes into the operational and technical aspects which can be universally applied. While there is merit and great benefits in the use of sophisticated technical packages that live off a common database and also integrate with one another, sadly often the prime emphasis becomes more one of mastering the system and promotes the tendency to live in a silo environment. As a result the importance tends to be focused on that single facet that the system serves rather than the broader picture. The fact that there is a relatively limited amount of material that generally describes the practice commonly known as retailing as an end to end process considering the enormous size of the industry is one of the motivating reasons for the documentation of this book.

## INTRODUCTION

### Retailing

Retailing is the offer of goods or services for sale by individuals or businesses to an end user. The channels by which these goods reach the final user may vary considerably and arrive via different sources such as wholesalers, trading houses or directly from the manufacturer and there are equally many differing variants in the way the goods are put on sale. Historically it is more likely that shopping would have been done at the village or town market, in a high street shop or at the "mom and pop" store which evolved over time into mass retailing stores that are often housed in shopping malls supported by smaller line shops.

More recently with the advent of the computer utilising various platforms such as the internet or social networks, shopping on line is growing exponentially using electronic payment methods with delivery via the post or with a courier man knocking on the front door of the customer bearing their purchase relatively shortly after the transaction has been processed.

The products that are put on offer will be determined by the demand to satisfy a need in the market place. Broadly the merchandise may be categorized into food stuffs, hard or durable goods such as appliances, furniture and electronics and soft goods that have a limited life span typically clothing, apparel and fabrics. Whatever the nature of the product, the key objective will be to acquire and sell the product at a price that will be more than it cost to bring it to the place of offer and thereby make a profit. Supporting activities such as the storage, movement of the goods, technology, and marketing will endeavour to ensure that the form, function and profit objective is maximised.

### The retail players

The saying "no man is an island" holds true in many spheres and this is certainly the case in the world of clothing retailing.

Various players, each with very different specialised skills are amalgamated together to deliver a completed outcome which is that of presenting product for sale to potential customers. These players are often very diverse not only in the activities that they perform but also in their personality traits which they possess. The key to a successful team is how maturely the interaction takes place and the mutual respect that every member has for each other's roles.

Below is a brief synopsis of the main player's roles and their dependency and integration with each other. The intimate details of the roles will be exposed in the future chapters as the science of retailing is explored in greater detail.

## THE PROCUREMENT TEAM

The foremost players in the clothing and apparel procurement team consist typically of the following members and are described in broad terms.

### Designers

Designers have a deep insight into the market they are targeting through the analysis of the changing trends and use these to provide creative direction and develop product designs for the buying teams to consider.

Usually these participants tend to think out of the box and their creative minds can challenge some of the comfort zones of other team members. What must be kept top of mind is that they need to consistently apply their intellect way ahead of time as to what they think the customer requires as opposed to their personal desires.

Typically the character traits which they will possess are that they are independent, spontaneous, extroverts, driven by ideas and are confident by nature.

Although the general perception of the word "designer" conjures up a vision of those who work at couture level, the reality is that it also includes those who are involved in creating ranges which may also be exclusive but will be more widely available and therefore can be considered as having been mass produced. Their choices will be influenced by the type of retailer they work for or the product category that they design for. The more traditional retailer which serves predominantly mature customers will be less influenced by radical fashion swings which in contrast will definitely affect the younger market's high fashion boutiques more rigorously.

Work is done at times under enormous pressure to meet critical deadlines, tough meeting schedules and involves frequent international travel. It is not surprising the perception is often one that they live a life of glory and glamour but contrary to this belief the reality is that it is not as extravagant as made out to be.

The fashion and trade shows, whether they be for yarn, fabric or garments are tiring affairs requiring hard work and stamina as is the shopping for appropriate samples, researching fashion magazines, the use of forecasting trend agencies, internet and blogs and out of all of this they need to possess the ability to then distil the emerging trends to create a storybook that will best suit their organisation's customer profiles.

The designer lives with the constant strain of knowing that their level of success will be measured by the eventual amount of money rung up at the till and getting the styling direction wrong or overextending the life of a particular look could have severe financial implications, especially in the cases where volumes are high.

The real challenge is to convince the buying teams and senior management to buy into their vision and have the confidence that what they have in mind will be commercially acceptable to the customer. The designer cannot ignore the technical aspects of the garment production as many problems can be evaded if these are taken cognisance of during the design process.

Retailers in the southern hemisphere do have the advantage that their seasons follow those of countries in the northern hemisphere which allows them to tap into the more successful designs that are trading in volume. However, with globalisation this is not always as clear cut as it was in previous years and the ability to follow as close to the season as possible requires techniques that facilitates the shortening of lead times and attempt to get the product to market as quickly as possible. The advent of communication technologies such as satellite television, internet and social media have brought exposure to different cultures, sports, films, lifestyles and trends such as those generated by specific events, health drives, environmental awareness and technology platforms that can have significant impacts on fashion which sometimes happen at very short notice.

A very important aspect is that the designer must adhere strictly to, is that of copyright. Instances have occurred that other competitor's garments are copied almost identically whether it be by style, print or design. Invariably the driving reason for this is the speed of being able to turn on a replica at a cheaper price. Although it may not be practical to register and copyright every design, any infringement can still be challenged and a consequence could occur of having the offending garments being removed from display and destroyed.

## Buyers

The buyer needs to have a clear understanding of the product that is required which is in line with the trend guidelines best suited to their target customer profiles, for both the high fashion segment as well as those that best serve the more traditional customer.

It is a fact is that the role of the designer and the buyer may be a bit blurred in that they research the same fashion forecasting sites and other sources of inspiration in order to put a range of garments together. Both roles must be aware of sizing, quality and costs related to fabrics, trimmings and production. To achieve this successfully they must be flexible enough to develop and buy the most suitable product that is in line with the prescribed strategy and achieves the desired profit margin in keeping with the set down targets. The evaluation of competitive activity and product ranges through regular store visits and comparative shopping provides the knowledge required to keep ahead of the field.

Effective communication and presentation skills are a prerequisite to brief and interact with suppliers as well as presenting product reviews to colleagues within their own group at all levels of seniority. With this comes the need to be able to accept criticism and resolve problems in a mature manner. The sad fact is that frequently when the analysis of the success of the range is evaluated at the end of the season, if the results are disappointing it is not uncommon for the buyer to shoulder the emotional burden of the poor performance. The truth of the matter is that the range was presented on more than one occasion to all team players including senior management all of whom signed the range off but in the final analysis they are more often than not, as is human nature, reluctant to be accept any proper accountability.

Coupled to ability to understand the wants of the customer is the sourcing of the most suitable supplier that will be selected for the specified product types in terms of their particular skills, technical ability, costing efficiency, attitude, transparency, honesty, focus on quality, communications and competitiveness while still meeting the ethical criteria that are acceptable to society.

A large part of the task will be to maintain good relations with suppliers, while at the same time being able to assertively negotiate prices with them and make sure the planned stocks are delivered on time. Communications need to be clear and specific to avoid disputes over issues which may arise through vague and confusing messages. For these reasons they need to be confident, take decisions based on results and be driven by a sense of urgency.

The buyer has to be multi-talented in that as well as being creative they also need to monitor the sales objectively and be flexible enough to react accordingly in terms of turning on or turning off production and transferring fabric and components to more appealing product styles where sales performance and fast emerging trends dictate.

What is key to be a successful buyer is the ability to work as part of the overall team and influence the rest of the team's activities which could be in the form of a managerial and developmental capacity that could also include both their peers and superiors.

The display of emotional maturity and commercial acumen within the controlled parameters as set by the merchandising arm in terms of the budgets, the number of product options and display space constraints is absolutely essential.

The same principle applies to the relationships that need to be maintained with the technical teams in regard to the use of the most appropriate fabrics which meet the product form and function demands in addition to ensuring that the brand standards of the garment are observed.

The fact that potentially the buyer together with the other retail players will be dealing with three to four seasons simultaneously at different stages for each season makes their task even more complicated. To clarify the phenomenon a bit further, the journey of this book attempts to describe the process from beginning to end for one season but while trading in the current season the thoughts and strategies are being developed and documented for two or possibly three seasons ahead followed by the range development leading up to the production taking place for next upcoming season.

The ability to absorb and interpret vast amounts of information from various sources, much of which originates from complex IT systems, can present a challenge to those who are not analytically minded.

Systems have altered the scope of the traditional buyer from being a pure "touchy feely art skill" to having to develop basic technical abilities through the continual emergence of innovative systems which have become a great advantage to the role.

Some buyer's, such as those for knitwear, ladies structured underwear, tailoring and footwear will require more expert fabric and garment construction knowledge of their respective industries in comparison to individuals who select the more straightforward cut, make and trim products such as dresses, blouses and casual trousers.

As the trade environment has become more global and through information technology development it is much faster, interactive and has enabled business to be done more effortlessly from a home base interacting with many different countries. A great deal of the job is done amongst many new emerging countries which has led to a need for urgency and nimbleness in order to locate the most effective plants that meet the quality requirements, be able to assess the required technical abilities, understand the economic and cultural demands of the respective countries as well as the logistical peculiarities and government regulations that may exist.

The sourcing of production has to take on different approaches as the pros and cons of dealing internationally needs to be carefully weighed up against those of dealing with the ever diminishing number of local suppliers. A critical factor is that suppliers must be ethical in terms of labour practices, remuneration, waste management, working conditions and safety. If such conditions are not met it is counter to the interests of the retailer to be associated with such suppliers from both a moral point of view and the exposure of malpractices could lead to negative media reports and the retailer will suffer the consequences that accompany such deeds. The measurement of performance is therefore key to gauging the effectiveness of suppliers.

In larger organisations a buyer will probably be supported by an assistant or trainee buyer who will normally be a person who wishes to pursue a career in the field. They will be largely responsible for the organisation of the ranges, perform some clerical work whilst preparing products for garment reviews, monitoring the product development critical path and production milestones, liaising with suppliers and technology as well as deputising for the buyer when they are out of the office.

A point to note is that the relationship between buyers and suppliers often develops into more than a pure business association due to the fact that they spend much time travelling together and working closely with one another building ranges. Close familiar relationships frequently make it difficult to maintain a business like association for the mutual benefit of both parties and can cloud business decision making and judgment. The temptation of bribery and incentives in exchange for placing large orders may be desirous. For newer naïve buyers the rule that the supplier is not your friend should be firmly applied simply because they are more easily seduced by grandiose lunches and gifts as many have unfortunately found out the hard way when they move on and are no longer of great importance to the particular supplier.

A way of balancing the workloads or ranking of buyers and merchandisers is to evaluate the actual number of suppliers, stock keeping units or barcodes being handled by each buyer and then make comparisons regarding workload and productivity of each buyer to established benchmarks.

## Merchandisers

The merchandiser or planner applies their focus on maximising profitability from the business end. This is done largely through the analysis of historical sales and the influence of the trend direction to determine the range categories and product breakdown within the overall sales budget.

The role defines what stock levels are required to meet the preset targets such as seasonal stock turnover or forward stock covers based on the sales trends over time. Knowing these requirements, the merchandiser will determine what intake or purchase quantities are needed at any point in time in the season for the total department and each product category.

The level of the budgets will determine the quantity of options in relation to styling, colour palette, size spans, pricing structure and levels of quality per category that will best service the customer for the time that the goods are expected be on offer prior to a new variety of product being introduced in line with the strategic predetermined seasonal themes.

The merchandiser's job has to be to provide guidance to the buyer to procure within the budget parameters. In short it can be described as providing the buyer with a shopping list or range plan that allows them to go out and fill in the blanks on the plan while buying product. This activity requires the careful management of the "open to buy" which can often be a source of tension between the buyer who always tends to want more and the merchandiser who holds the purse strings. A good deal of emotional maturity and teamwork on both sides is therefore critical for a successful partnership.

Sadly the merchandising role is often branded as a dull, boring number crunching task in accordance with mathematical calculations and while it is this, it can be better described as a creative manipulation of numbers. This task is highly rewarding when positive trade results are achieved or alternatively equally as depressing when these do not materialise. The role can be likened to that of a husband who places his entire salary on a dead cert horse at the races which was by no means appreciated by his wife. However when the horse won he was similarly unpopular for not putting more money on the horse!

Like the buying role, the merchandiser deals with different activities simultaneously as part of the team across a number of seasons and therefore requires high levels of multi-tasking and re-prioritising in the forward planning, problem resolution, critical milestone management, analysis and timeous action implementation.

As the actual trade takes place the results need to be carefully analysed and immediate action plans initiated in order to maximise the opportunities and minimise the levels of markdowns that erode the profits. For these reasons they need to be logical, reliable, and consistent in order to take decisions based on fact.

The regular timeous generation of reports detailing sales analysis, stock levels and forward planning needs are distributed to all team members and to senior management. Often numeric information and commercial analysis is demanded on an immediate ad-hoc basis which adds pressure to the job function and can be very disruptive to routines which in such situations requires the merchandiser to adapt quickly and effectively.

The merchandiser plays an integral role during the presentation at product reviews from the numbers perspective which influences the agreed product mix and justification of the levels of sales budgets.

A detailed understanding is necessary of the stores and the customer profile inherent to respective stores that are best met through the attributes of the ranges in terms of styling, colour and size that are put on offer within the store space constraints. The task is best described by the saying "plan each store as if it is your own" which could never be truer.

With sophisticated IT development and the availability of various software packages, some of which may be developed exclusively for the retailer, will provide quick sales analysis, production planning and afford the ability to make sound decisions based on accurate data. This information is especially necessary to give guidance to the allocator or distributor who will be sending the appropriate quantities to satisfy the store's needs as well as give direction as to the level of repeat buys for products that are trading above expectations.

Some organisational structures do differentiate the allocation function between the merchandiser who focuses on the forecasting and production planning and that of the allocator or location planner who will be responsible to distribute the product to the stores in the most appropriate combinations of styles, colour and sizes that meet the store profiles. This function can be housed as an extension within the buying division or may be part of a separate centralised group where an allocator may be responsible for a diverse number of departments. The benefits of such a centralised structure is that there could be a cost saving advantage especially where smaller departments do not warrant a dedicated staff member but added to this is a pool of knowledge which develops a highly skilled team who are able to cross pollinate information, coordinate inter departmental promotions effectively and develop consistent techniques and skills. The identification of common emerging trends will contribute to the optimisation of sales and assist in the control of stock quantities at a very detailed level and thereby maximise profits. Close connections to the departmental merchandisers is maintained to ensure that their actions are aligned to the departmental strategy and plans.

The need for the diversification of the function also makes more sense from the point of view in that where the distribution function is retained within the department it inevitably adds to the increasing workload of the merchandiser. The departmental merchandiser task has more and more been impacted on by the development, the implementation and mastering of complex and sophisticated information systems that analyse sales and stock with added forward planning functionalities.

Many such systems are able to integrate with other supporting IT platforms such as supplier performance, technological measurement, critical path management, ordering, logistical and store systems. The added management of a complex allocation system that is necessary to move the stock to stores is more and more difficult with the result that the incumbent is in danger of being drawn into concentrating on and coping with the intricate detail. As a result, the merchandiser runs the risk of losing sight of the bigger objectives as set out in the strategy and operational plans and the consequent degrading of the inherent merchant intuition becomes very real.

The merchandiser needs to effectively manage and develop the merchandising team which can, not unlike the buying role, consist of an assistant merchandiser or trainee who aspire to be a merchandiser.

The role ensures cohesion of activities that have to be synchronized based on actual sales performance through the formalised interaction with other stakeholders such as the buyers and technologists. This contact is usually in the form of regular, typically weekly, departmental meetings where corrective decisions and plans of action are agreed. Frequent association with the points of sale in stores through written communications and reports as well as formal site visits are critical to keep aligned with the customer's preferences and emerging trends and confirm that the stores are sharing the same vision of the overall strategy.

The need to guide suppliers assertively in terms of prioritisation and the achievement of deadlines is critical to meet the suitable stock requirements at any point in time, particularly in relation to peak seasonal periods or key events. For example, once winter breaks, which it does every year except the exact date is not easy to predict, the objective is to have the right stocks in place such as knitwear, thermal underwear, scarves and the like in sufficient quantities to meet the rush. The usual manner to assist in the anticipation of the weather trend is done through reference to previous years data when the weather changes happened which also help to understand variations in out of ordinary performance at particular times. The challenge is therefore to have the appropriate quantities in the stores at the vital time while the maintenance of the balance of stocks must be adequate to cater for the demand without overstocking the stores ahead of planned stock targets. Events such as Easter, Christmas, Valentine's Day and Mother's day are easier to predict and the right levels of stock can be made more accurately available at the right time.

Where suppliers do not meet the required delivery dates, the merchandiser needs to manage the consequences that have to be applied for the underperformance. This can result in some very sensitive and emotional discussions and the negotiation of penalties typically in the form of discounts, sale or return agreements or even total cancellation which will no doubt impact negatively on both parties.

## Technology

Technical Teams consist broadly of the fabric and garment technologists. Fabric technologists are highly trained specialists who focus on typically woven or knitted disciplines. Specialised products such as knitwear, tailoring and footwear require added knowledge of components and specific production machinery.

A major portion of the fabric technologist's task is the development and innovation of new fabrics and the enhancement of existing products. New fibres and blends of fibres such as the blending of natural and synthetic fibres, addition of chemicals to finishing process will possibly lead to new inventions and improvements such as better washability, softer handles, easy care properties like easy to iron, crease resistant finishes, rot resistant applications, seamless or seams that are glued that allow for smoother looks particularly for under garments, the evolvement of elastane products such as lycra which revolutionised active and casual wear and the enhancement of thermal properties of winter undergarments. The success of such developments which add to the profitability as well as the form and function necessitates a close working relationship with suppliers, mills and value adders.

Garment technology have the responsibility to ensure that the make-up of the garment meets the set down criteria and the componentry like buttons, interlinings and threads are of the standard that is functional and are not inferior.

Many factories have developed specified technological capabilities that have been built around the production of a particular category of garments relevant to them which vary from factory to factory or even within the same plant. The garment technologist must understand this implicitly and exploit this knowledge to its fullest.

The relationship with the commercial team is sometimes strained as the ideal level of form and function can be challenged by the need to market the product at the most commercially competitive price.

The objective of the garment technologist is to ensure that quality is not compromised. The tasks essential to achieve this can be varied, for example, the assessment of potential manufacturers and fabric mills to ensure that the established standards are achievable, the specification of raw materials, overseeing sampling stages and ensuring that any delays which may result through the process do not compromise the delivery prerequisites.

In safeguarding that the all quality standards are met particularly through the inspection of garments, inspectors need to possess specific skills. Quality controllers should be ethical, sincere and honest, open mindedly being willing to consider alternatives, be diplomatic and tactful in their dealings with people and are able to actively observe their surroundings as well as perceive and adapt to varying situations.

The technologist has an intimate knowledge of the supplier base through historical awareness as well as from continually researching new and existing suppliers. As the sourcing specialist they have to guide buying teams in the selection of the most appropriate manufacturer for the various types of product. It is also very essential that they are conscious of the fabric prominence for the forthcoming season as dictated by the strategies and budget levels to ensure that there is sufficient capacities at the relevant mills to meet the overall demands without compromising quality.

The task of assessing potentially new suppliers is a role that may be included in the stable of the technical team or it may be hived off to defined sourcing specialists who are knowledgeable team members that recognise the strengths and weaknesses of suppliers and based on this where best to place orders accordingly.

Suppliers are assessed on various criteria such as their management infrastructure, financial stability, specialised equipment availability, fabric specialty, levels of innovation, fashion or basic production orientation, the other retailers they serve, their flexibility of cost negotiability and social responsibility policies. Other external factors that may well influence the selection of suppliers could be those like prevailing exchange rates, remuneration policies and physical locality.

In summary, the significance must be emphasised that the diverse buying teams all have to have a clear informed understanding of each other's roles and priorities and that they are aligned to ensure all their tasks are integrated to achieve the goal of delivering consistent quality products manufactured by appropriately skilled suppliers on time all the time. This is especially imperative in the case of more complex products such as corsetry, tailored garments and knitwear.

The handling, packaging, storage and movement of the product through the supply channels has to be done in such a way that the quality of the product is not allowed to deteriorate in any way whatsoever. As some product is sourced from more distant locations a newer trend is to contract the technical function out to approved independent technical service providers or to trusted garment and fabric suppliers themselves who understand and are committed to the standards required. These service providers are thereby able to approve samples, perform quality control and be responsible for the eventual release of the finished product.

## BUYING GROUP ORGANISATION

A characteristic merchandise hierarchical organisational structure of a retailer is illustrated below where mainstream buying and merchandising function cascades down from the highest platform to the lower department level details. Service areas as depicted on the right hand side of the diagram support the core functions.

*Typical buying group organisation chart*

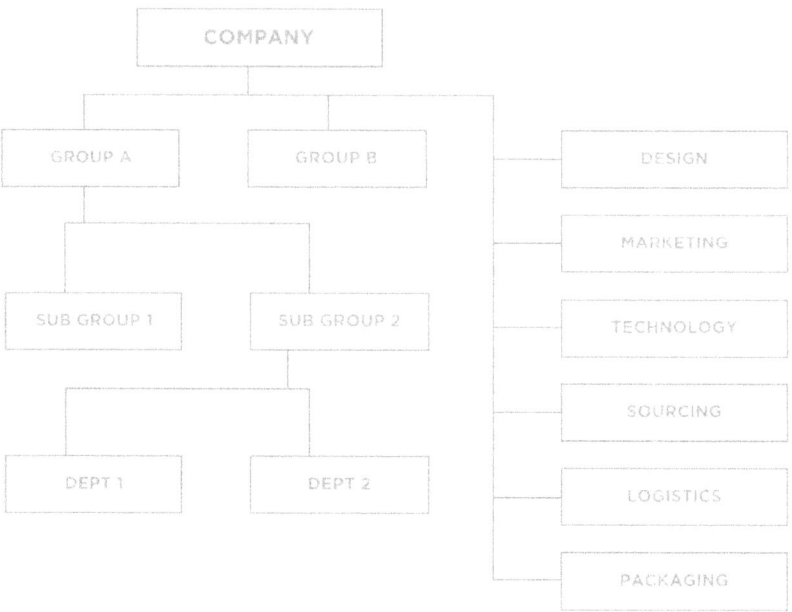

The basic hierarchical staffing roles of all the key players in a mainstream buying structure is outlined diagrammatically below.

The chief executive officer is clearly the leader together with the board of directors who ensure that the overall company strategic intent is delivered and the profits are achieved as reward to the shareholders to whom they are accountable.

Group executives look after the broad category types such as menswear, ladieswear and childrenswear. The responsibility is to ensure that the group delivers to the set strategy and is reacting properly to changing trading conditions while still meeting the profit objective.

Within the mainstream groups such as menswear a sub division into sub groups may well take place probably by lifestyle such as formal wear and casual wear. The category manager is responsible for the mini business or sub group with set turnover targets, profit objectives and strategies.

Buyers, merchandisers and location planners operate at the departmental level down to the lowest degree of product being colour and size and are responsible that the management of the detail delivers the eventual goals at all the higher levels.

*Key staffing hierarchy posts of a buying organisation*

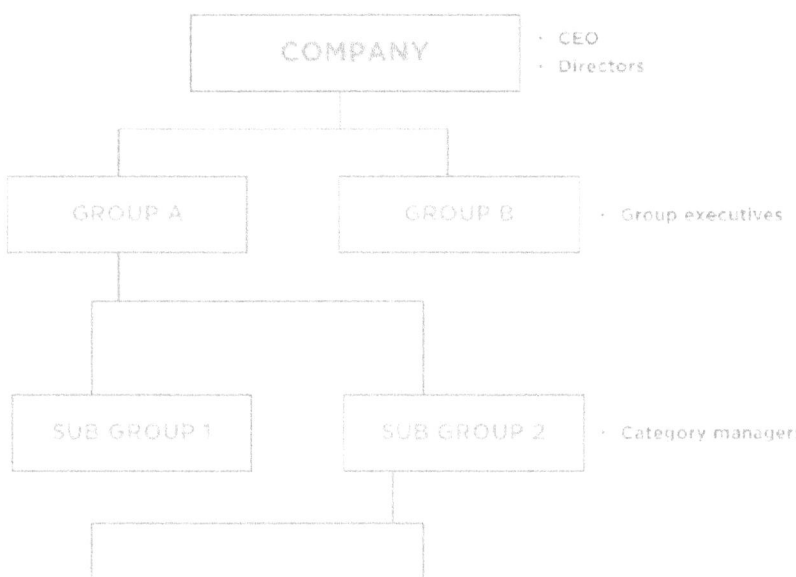

## MERCHANDISE ARITHMETIC

The main purpose of merchandise planning is to forecast sales for the period under review and manage the levels of stock in the correct assortments based on the historical performance and forward trends. Buyers are guided to procure within the parameters of the budget and ensure that the right product is delivered to the right stores in the right quantities of style, colours and size in order to maximise the sales and profit objectives and minimise mark downs. In order that this is done effectively it is important that the numerical planning is done accurately and is able to be measured in line with a set of predetermined criteria.

It is a known fact that things do not always go according to plan so it is equally important to measure the actual performance against what was originally envisaged and recommend corrective action where deviations occur. This may take various forms whether it is buying more of a style if possible, turning off supply or converting styles into those that are more in demand. Allocation quantities need to be reviewed in line with the individual store performances. These actions need to be done as urgently as possible after the analysis is completed.

Key performance indicators

For stakeholders to be able to check whether the performance is on track to achieve the strategic objectives it is measured against a suite of pre-set performance indicators. The most common performance pointers which are assigned targets that will deliver the desired financial requirements, are the following.

Sales

Markdowns

Buying margin

Sales margin

Stock forward cover

Stock annual turn

Return on inventory investment

It is absolutely imperative that these indicators are clearly understood by all members of the retail team both in the head office and stores and what role they play in the support of them. The measures are almost always referred to in financial reports as shareholders utilise these to determine their level of confidence in the company performance.

## Business acumen

In order that the profit motives are achieved effectively it is imperative that all team players have an acceptable measure of business acumen. Many decisions made at any level are often of substandard quality through the misinterpretations of basic business formulae and concepts. Clarity through the understanding of retail arithmetic makes life less confusing with less disruption and improved productivity in the generation of profits.

Business acumen can be described as the entrepreneurial ability to improve results through focusing on the customer, applying the knowledge of the business and being aware of the external market environment and competitors.

*All vital performance indicators are underpinned by the fundamental building blocks of sales, markdowns, Intake and stock which may be illustrated diagrammatically that highlights the MERCHANT and FINANCIAL kpi's as follows.*

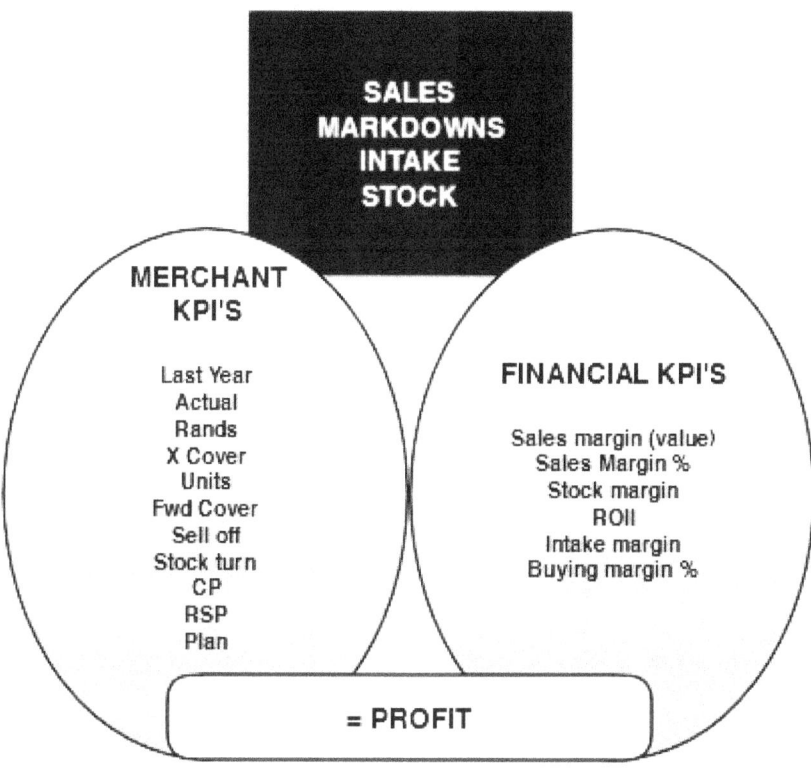

 A brief explanation of each one of the key performance indicators as well as how they are derived is outlined as follows.

## Sales

are recorded and planned in monetary value although reference is frequently made to volumes in order to plan production capacity requirements. The monetary value measurement is expressed as a percentage in relation to another value which is normally against the comparable sales of the previous year or against the budgeted sales for the corresponding current period. The measurement within the stores can also be done such as the takings per square metre to assist in the apportionment of amount of display space deserved by product categories within the departments. Sales per square metre also serve as a benchmark target to which minimum performance is required to assess the viability of carrying particular ranges and is a good measure which can be referenced by the buying teams when probing the sales performance of product in stores. It should be understood that various designs of display equipment such as wall displays, racks and tables are also apportioned varying relative square metreage rates.

## Growth percentages

compared to other periods are used to identify problems or successes in buying, product flow, inventory levels, merchandising, and advertising assessment. These can be better understood where there is distortion due to changes in the environment such as selling space expansion or store closures, competitive activity and out of the ordinary events.

The calculation of the growth percentage is the method of expressing the difference between two values such as this year and last year sales divided by the total sales for the same period. Alternatively the measurement of growth can also be compared to the set targets which is particularly relevant in the sense that the historical data may be flawed and the fact the business is planned against set targets and should these be deviated from a more accurate corrective adjustment can take place.

$$\text{GROWTH \%} = \frac{TY - LY}{LY} \times 100$$

Assume last year sales was 700 and this year sales are 900. The sales growth would therefore be [(900-700)/900] x 100=22.2%

The desired sales level can also be derived by applying a percentage increase.

Assume a percentage increase of 10% is required against last year and the sales for last year is 700. The required sales budget for this year will therefore be 700 x 1.10=770

It should be noted that in terms of percentage growth a differentiation should be made between overall growth where the total increase of the department includes all products in contrast to a like for like increase which is between identical products from the corresponding season in the previous year and represents a true inflationary measurement.

The common opinion is that the achievement of this measure is the crucial to ensure the delivery of the other key indicators.

## Contribution percentage

is the way of expressing in monetary or unit value as a percentage that a component represents of the whole. The use of this measurement is frequently used to compare performances or to extrapolate in the future planning scenarios at any level of the hierarchy.

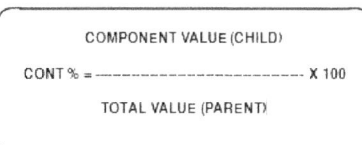

Assume a department (parent) consists of four products (children) a tabular illustration below shows what contribution % the sales of each product represents.

| DEPT ABC | SALES | % CONT |
|---|---|---|
| PRODUCT A | 60 000 | 24% |
| PRODUCT B | 35 000 | 14% |
| PRODUCT C | 75 000 | 30% |
| PRODUCT D | 80 000 | 32% |
| TOTAL | 250 000 | 100% |

## Markdowns

are inevitable in some form or other. The requirement to reduce merchandise can be due to various reasons such as sales being below expectation, the need to clear stock due to necessity and allowing the management of the pipeline to facilitate newness to flow through and also to be able to contain stocks within the parameters of the set stock targets. Markdowns need to be provided for by way of a budget in spite of it being difficult to predict the exact nature of the markdown at the lower levels of product.

The markdown value is the monetary value by which the product was reduced.

PRICE AT OLD RSP - PRICE AT NET RSP X UNITS

= MARK DOWN VALUE

Markdowns are measured in percentage terms derived by the relationship of the markdown value to the total retail sales for the period.

MARKDOWN % =

$$\text{MARKDOWN } \% = \frac{\text{MARKDOWN VALUE}}{\text{ORIGINAL RSP VALUE}} \times 100$$

Assume for the period the value of markdown was 1000 and the corresponding sales were 10000. The markdown percentage would therefore be

(1000/10000) x 100=10%

The size of the provision for markdown is dependent on historical data and the acceptable percentage in relation to the original sales budget or a retail selling price. The levels of markdown will vary dependent on the nature of the product.

Typically the more high fashion type product such as ladies tops will have a higher markdown percentage to sales which can be as high as fifteen percent while the very basic product that is sold as a continuity item rather than a single input such as underwear will be much lower and may even only be done routinely to flush older merchandise out of the system. In order to cater for these variances the buying margin policy for the various categories will accordingly reflect these levels of risk.

Product is generally marked down on the go or alternatively the affected goods are removed from display until a planned seasonal sale which may be two or three times per annum. The main reason for higher levels of markdown is most often that the customer rejects the offer through disillusionment or when the most popular colour or size is not available. Fragmentation of ranges inevitably slows the rate of sale and consequently results in displays becoming untidy and disorganised as well as restricting the display space required for new lines. Space constraints often lead to the product being removed from display never to see the light of day again until the major seasonal sale.

Depending on the overall demand for fragmented pockets of stock it may be considered to recall all the odds back to a facility where the goods can be consolidated. New sets of availability are then reported and the goods are redistributed to a limited catalogue of stores that have previously sold the goods at an acceptable level. The risk of this practice is the additional costs which are incurred in handling, transport, repacking, reallocation and redistribution while the goods are still relevant must be such that a profit benefit is still returned. Invariably it is seldom the option that will be selected.

It is not uncommon to pack away seasonal product such as thermal underwear. Winter hosiery, swimwear at the end of the season and bring them back to the display units from storage at the commencement of the next season. The shortcoming is that the stock that is re-introduced is often tatty, discoloured and may even be shop soiled and lacking the crispness of fresh goods. If this practice is done it is advisable to return them to a value add facility where they can be repackaged and correctly price marked for the new season before re-introducing the goods back into the system.

There are various options as how to deal with reductions. The most commonly used one is that where the goods are marked down on a continual basis during the trading season. This has the downside that it causes a distraction from new ranges and themes as well as can damage the brand integrity in the eye of the customer. The consumers also tend to adjust their buying patterns in the knowledge that the goods will inevitably be cleared at a lower price at some time in the near future and will wait for these occurrences to happen rather than pay the full price. The alternative possibility is to withdraw the affected goods from display until the next specific seasonal sale.

Some chains may have designated stores where sale and distressed goods are combined and sold at reduced prices. Another route that may be followed is to off load the merchandise to jobbers or resellers at very low prices but in both cases this requires added handling as well as the removal of labelling whilst at the same time incurring additional associated costs.

## Markup percentage

is described as the percentage of the cost price that is added to the cost price to derive the selling price. The key difference between the mark up and the margin is that the percentage is based on cost while margins are based on sales. It is therefore true to say that a selling price with a 30% margin results in more profit than a selling price with a 30% mark up on the cost price.

$$\text{MARK UP \%} = \frac{\text{SELLING VALUE - COST VALUE}}{\text{COST VALUE}} \times 100$$

## Margins

are an indicator of performance relative to certain key measures in the business (usually stock and sales) expressed in monetary terms or as a %. The target margins are set in strategy and Kpi's reviews.

## Buying margin

is the margin at which the goods were purchased and is often referred to as the primary margin. This margin is expressed as a percentage and equates to the selling value less the cost value expressed as a percentage of the selling value.

$$\text{BUY MARGIN \%} = \frac{\text{SELL VAL - COST VAL}}{\text{SELL VAL}} \times 100$$

Assume that sales budget for the period is 350 000 and the cost value of the goods purchased is 160 000.

The buying margin is therefore 350000−160000=190000

The buying margin percentage equates to [(350000-160000)/350000] x100=54.3%

The margin is a part of the strategic plan and while there is an overall target for the company. The margins at the lower levels will vary and will be largely dependent on the fashionability and volume factor of the product. It may also be strategically different in the sense that a product may be sold at a low or even no margin to gain a competitive advantage and thereby increase market share. As the achievement of the buying or intake margin is critical to the negotiation process it is absolutely essential that it is closely monitored during the procurement process to ensure that the achievement of the overall target margin remains on track.

## Sales margin

in monetary value is the difference between the actual sales value which is registered at the till and the total cost of the goods sold which includes factors such as markdowns. It should be noted that the cost value of each intake may differ so the cost value will be the weighted combination of the various costs or quantities.

$$\text{SALES MARGIN (MONETRY)} = \text{SALES - COST OF GOODS SOLD}$$

The margin is expressed as a percentage and refers to the relationship between sales and cost value and the total sales expressed as a percentage.

$$\text{SELL MARGIN \%} = \frac{\text{SALES - COST OF GOODS SOLD}}{\text{SALES}} \times 100$$

* Cost of goods sold = Sales margin

Assume that the sales for the period are 200 000 and the cost of the goods sold (including added costs to the base cost of the garment) are 130 000.

The Sales Margin will therefore be 200000−130000=70000

The Sales Margin % will be (70000/200000) X 100=35%

*An example of the derivation of the weighted cost value is illustrated in the following diagram*

The variance of the anticipated sales volumes that were used to determine the buying margin may well be very different to volume proportions that are actually sold and therefore will ultimately deliver a different aggregated sales margin.

The sales margin target is determined by the intake margin after taking expected markdowns into account and has the same logical relationship between the sales value and cost value expressed as a percentage. The difference however is that the actual sales value which is achieved can be very different. It is therefore key to carefully observe what was expected to happen to what actually happened and make sure that is kept in mind when determining forward predictions.

Other factors that may well influence the accuracy of sales margins may well be instances such as

Incorrect RSVP or cost prices

Incorrect ticketing

High returns to manufacturers

Different shopping patterns to that what was expected in that they may purchase more low margin items

The turning on or turning off of merchandise which affect the balance of margins

## Weighted retail selling prices

is where in determining the overall average selling price for a department it takes into account the volumes of each component with varying retail selling prices rather than the straight average calculation using the number of components.

*This is best illustrated as follows in the example below*

| UNITS SOLD | RSP | SALES VALUE | AVERAGE RSP | WEIGHTED AVERAGE RSP |
|---|---|---|---|---|
| 1000 | 100.00 | 100 000 | (100+150+ 200) | (100000+ 750000+ 500000) |
| 5000 | 150.00 | 750 000 | | |
| 2500 | 200.00 | 500 000 | 3 | 8500 |
| 8500 | | 1 350 000 | 150.00 | 158.82 |

## Inflation

can only be truly measured by comparing product which is identical or extremely similar from one year to the next and is therefore described as like on like inflation.

## Price movement

applies to the entire basket of products of a department which may be different in terms of styling, fabric and componentry is included in the determination of the overall change in price across the various pricing categories will indicate the extent by which a departments prices total as an average (including the like for like inflation products) have moved from the one year to the next.

*Below is an illustrative diagramme outlining the effect of changing volumes from one year to the next on the overall price movement where a price increase of 10% is applied?*

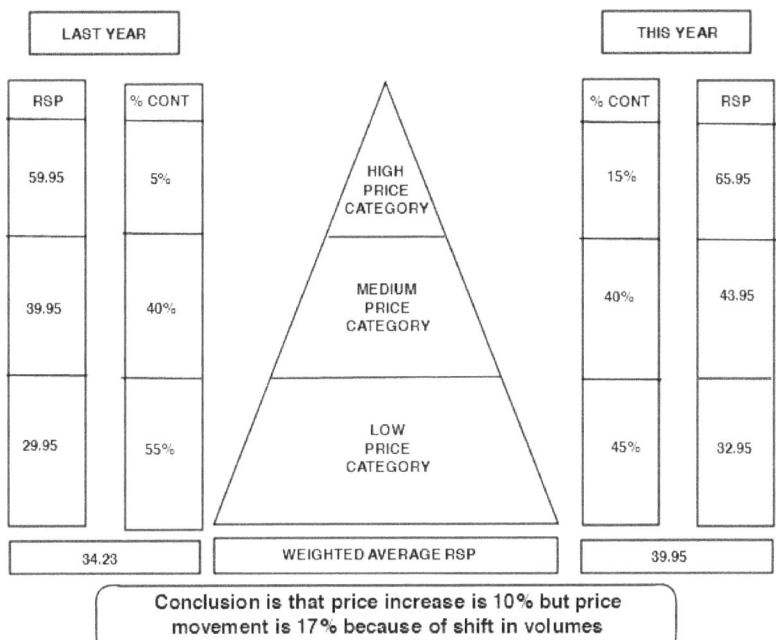

| LAST YEAR | | | THIS YEAR | |
|---|---|---|---|---|
| **RSP** | **% CONT** | | **% CONT** | **RSP** |
| 59.95 | 5% | HIGH PRICE CATEGORY | 15% | 65.95 |
| 39.95 | 40% | MEDIUM PRICE CATEGORY | 40% | 43.95 |
| 29.95 | 55% | LOW PRICE CATEGORY | 45% | 32.95 |
| 34.23 | | WEIGHTED AVERAGE RSP | 39.95 | |

Conclusion is that price increase is 10% but price movement is 17% because of shift in volumes

## Monetary value in relation to unit volume

A critical point to note is that while the average RSVP may change significantly and result in an increase above inflation, the net effect would be an increase in margin but the end result would be a reduction in units compared to the previous year and consequently would hamper the ability of the department to service the catalogue as effectively as the previous year. The converse will be experienced where the RSVP is reduced assuming the same budget level is maintained.

The qualification needs to be made that the if the end objective is profit in monetary value it stands to reason that in principle budgeted sales are set in financial terms as opposed to unit terms.

As an example assume the following

Last year a product sold 250 000 units per month at 29.95 which would return sales of 7.5 million

If the price is reduced to 24.95 the probability is that the volume per month will increase to 275 000 per month which would deliver a monetary sale of 6.9 million.

The conclusion is that even though the units at the lower RSVP increase, the actual revenue is less.

## Stock forward cover

is the amount of stock required at any one point in time that will permit the forward sales budgets to be achieved. The measurement is typically in weeks and can be expressed as the amount of weeks that is based on the sales plan over the time that it will take for the stock to be exhausted.

Stock levels will essentially be higher or lower over time depending on seasonal trends, promotional launches, markdown activities and holiday events. The fluctuations will be reflected in the sales plans and as a result the inventory level will fall and rise in empathy to the sales plan. The target number of weeks can remain reasonably consistent throughout the year and will really only need to be adjusted where situations deem it necessary such as for factory closures over holiday periods and in the event of build up for new initiative launches such as store openings.

The appropriate number of weeks selected will be determined based on historical data, the strategy intents and the nature of the product. Properties such as fashionability, amount of sizes, lead times from supplier for replenishment, the number of deliveries and turnover of individual stores will have an influence over the number of weeks cover chosen. Commonly the more fashionable the merchandise is, the lesser the number of weeks will be required as the time it is on offer may well be shorter before the next input of new replacement styles in comparison to the basic continuity commodities.

Larger outlets stock tend to sell out at a quicker rate and have greater volumes of sales and therefore are able to survive on less weeks cover compared to the smaller stores with smaller turnovers which demand a less frequent replenishment and consequently require more weeks cover in order that full availability of all colours and sizes are on offer at any one point in time.

The proximity of stores to the replenishment centres will also have an influence on the stockholding requirements and invariably the rural stores far from the distribution points may receive less frequent deliveries which take longer to reach them and subsequently these stores will have to have more weeks cover than their relations in the city centres who are closer to the distribution centres.

The principle, however, remains to keep the forward cover as low as possible in order that the stock will be replaced more regularly and thereby is able to generate profit more frequently.

> WEEKS FORWARD COVER =
>
> CLOSING STOCK - SUM OF FORWARD WEEKS SALES

Assume at a point in time the stock holding is 900

The forward sales per weeks going forward are 150, 200, 130, 100, 120, 110, 90,110,140, and so on...

The number of weeks that the 900 worth of stock will last before running out will be

900= 150+200+130+100+120+110+90

This will therefore represent 7 weeks forward cover of stock required to achieve targeted sales.

The forward cover is a key measurement to determine the stock turn of the business on an annual and seasonal basis needs to take into account

The amount of stock that can be held on the sales floor at any one point in time

The amount of stock that can be held at outside storage facilities

The time that goods are in transit to stores

The type of merchandise as to whether it is fashion or continuity inputs

The type of supply chain which may be warehoused or delivered directly ex supplier

The ability to finance the cost of catalogue

Any specific risks that may be involved in holding and transit of stock such as shelf life

## Times cover

is in no way related to forward cover but represents the speed that goods are selling in stores and is reflected in weeks and is seen as a relativity measure between stores in terms of the sales to stock ratios.

The formula to determine the times cover is

$$\frac{\text{OPEN STOCK FOR THE PERIOD}}{\text{AVERAGE SALES FOR THE PERIOD}}$$

Assume the opening stock for January is 2500 in order to calculate the sales to stock ratio for the 4 weeks of January is done as follows

Sales for January = 340+250+190+200 = 980

Average sales = 980/4 = 245

Times cover = 2500/245

$\qquad$ = 10.2 weeks

In other words the stock will all be sold out in 10.2 weeks if nothing else is received during the month.

It should be distinguished that that this is seen as a more instantaneous measure to highlight anomalies to alert the need to implement further investigation as it assumes that the rate of sales going forward will be the same as the past.

## Stock annual turn

is the number of times the stock inventory is sold and replaced in the year. The year is based on a moving 52 actual weeks and therefore does not have a start and end date.

$$\frac{\text{CUMULATIVE SALES FOR THE LAST 52 WEEKS}}{\text{MOVING AVERAGE STOCK}}$$

Each time this happens, profit is generated and therefore the more times this occurs the more times a profit is delivered.

Stock annual turn is usually expressed as the cumulative sales for the previous fifty two weeks divided by the average stock holding for the same period.

Assuming the cumulative sales for the preceding 52 weeks (annual) is 60 000 and the average stock for the period is 15 000 then the stock turn will be 60000/15000 = 4 times.

There is a direct link to stock forward cover value as the lower the number of weeks are, the less the average stock holding will be and as a result the higher the stock turn will be. A point to note about the relationship is that the forward cover can be determined from the stock turn value or vice versa.

$$\text{FORWARD COVER} = \frac{52}{\text{STOCK TURN}}$$

The forward cover can be determined from the stock turn value by dividing the forward cover number of weeks into 52 weeks.

If stock turn is 6 then forward cover will be 52/6 = 8.7 weeks

$$\text{STOCK TURN} = \frac{52}{\text{FORWARD COVER}}$$

Conversely, if forward cover is 9 weeks then stock turn will be 52/9 = 5.8 times

The significance of the non-achievement of the target stock turn can result in the accumulation of higher seasonal stocks which will inevitably be destined for the reduction counters as it will no longer be seasonally relevant and will probably look fatigued and fragmented. The intake of the new seasonal ranges will also be choked in order to remain within the stock parameters. The downside for those retailers who rely on the quicker turn of stock to enable a return which facilitates the payment of goods within the payment terms timeline is that if this is not realised it will have a negative effect on the availability of ready cash or liquidity. The consequence is that the inventory is carried for longer periods of time and the payment of goods before they are sold enforces higher interest charges to finance the holding of goods.

*In order to illustrate the effectiveness of the level of stock turn this can be done by the following hypothetical example of playing the one arm bandit gaming machines in the following diagram.*

It therefore stands to reason that the higher the stock turn is of a product the more likely it will have a lower margin than a product that has a high margin but turns stock less frequently. This is clearly evidenced by the nature of goods that are marketed.

*Diagrammatically the relationship between turn and margin can be illustrated as below*

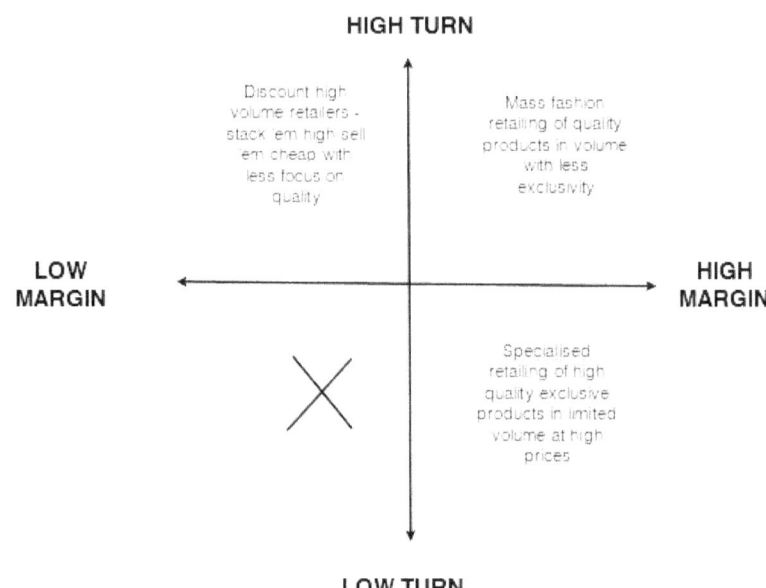

## Sell off percentage

is defined as the percentage of stock available to be sold within a designated period. The term is also often referred to as the clearance or sell through percentage which indicates how well the stock is being sold.

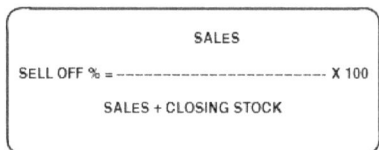

$$SELL\ OFF\ \% = \frac{SALES}{SALES + CLOSING\ STOCK} \times 100$$

Assume that there are sales for a product for a set period of 40 units which has a closing stock of 160 units at the end of the period.

The resultant sell off % will be 40/ (40+160) x 100 = 20%

While this measurement is glibly used there are pitfalls that need to be avoided to ensure that as a relativity measure apples are not being compared to pears. To avoid this the following set up must be in place:

The period for the products being compared is exactly the same.

There must be full availability of the products during the period from the start which means there are no sell outs or any additional or late intake during the period.

The amount of stock should be considered as low stock levels may deliver a flattering sell off. For example if there are only two units and one is sold the selloff % is 50% which is great but it is only one unit.

It is therefore a dangerous measure in isolation and each result should be considered with the view of "it depends".

## Average per store
is a measure which enables the assessment of the number of units being sold per week by store of a department, category or product in relation to other stores and thereby draw conclusions.

$$\text{TOTAL SALES FOR PERIOD} \over \text{NUMBER OF WEEKS}$$

Suppositions that may be drawn are

Are the sales at an acceptable rate to justify the cataloguing of a store?

Provides a dip stick view of the potential of a product in other stores.

Allows comparison across groups and stores.

Provides comparison of actual sales against targets that were bought against.

## Shrinkage percentage
reflects the percentage of sales lost to shrinkage or wastage and the result is measured against set targets to deem whether or not they are acceptable.

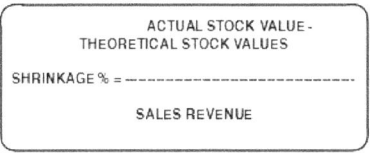

$$\text{SHRINKAGE \%} = \frac{\text{ACTUAL STOCK VALUE} - \text{THEORETICAL STOCK VALUES}}{\text{SALES REVENUE}}$$

The cause of shrinkage is caused by both internal and external factors such as employee theft and paperwork errors and damaged merchandise write offs. External causes are usually pilferage and undetected errors by suppliers.

## Return on inventory investment (ROII)

is the measure of the amount of return that is received for the investment in stock.

The profit productivity of the stock depends on the number of times the inventory is sold and replaced and the more frequent these spells are the more times it will generate a profit. The relationship of the cumulative monetary sales margin value for the period being measured to the average cost value of stock will deliver the number of times profit was made.

The average cost of the stock is determined by the opening stock at the beginning of the period being measured and is added to the stock values per month which is divided by the number of months.

$$\frac{\text{PROGRESSIVE SALES MARGIN (VALUE)}}{\text{AVERAGE COST OF STOCK}}$$

Accept the period being measured is six months and the total sales margin value is 3000. The opening cost value stock of 1000 added to the stock holdings of each of the six months and divided by the number of months plus 1. This value divided into the total sales margin will deliver the number of times profit was generated.

Average cost of stock = 1000 + (900+800+1100+1200+1000+900) =6900/7=985.7

ROII will be 3000/985.7=3.0

Techniques to improve the return on investments will include

Run effective promotions regularly

Reduce the average stock holdings by buying more frequently and weigh up bulk discounts and minimum order quantities very carefully

At times it is preferable to negotiate longer credit terms with the supplier in order to reduce the stock investment by the sales before payment has to be made

Consider the viability of offering a product for sale if the return is low

Set reasonable stock turns for items and work towards achieving an inventory position that returns similar turns for each item in the category

Remove un acceptable underperforming items from display prior to markdon

Interdependency of performance indicators

The importance of recognising the interdependence of the performance indicators is paramount.

Should the sales target be under achieved, in all probability the margin targets will not have sufficient sales value to be realised, the stock cover will be higher due to the unsold stock and therefore the stock turn will decrease as will the return on inventory investment.

If the markdowns are higher than originally planned, the margin targets and return on inventory investment will consequently be under achieved.

When the stock sells in different proportions to what was expected and where the products have differential margins, the overall aggregated margin could well deliver a different result to what was anticipated. For example, this phenomenon will occur if sales of loss leading low margin goods exceed budgets and perhaps the higher fashion high margin products sell less than hoped for.

The non-achievement of stock forward cover targets means that the stock annual turns will not be attained and consequently the sales and markdown expectations may or may not be accomplished depending on the severity of the deviation but undoubtedly there will certainly be a resultant impact on the return of inventory investment.

The return on inventory investment will not be realised if any one of the other targets are not achieved.

*By means of a matrix the interdependence of the performance indicators may be shown as follows*

Note that if the individual performance indicators in the left hand column are not achieved the crosses in the row to the corresponding performance indicators under the relevant headings will also be negatively impacted.

| | SALES | MARKDOWNS | BUYING MARGIN | SALES MARGIN | STOCK FORWARD COVER | STOCK ANNUAL TURN | ROII |
|---|---|---|---|---|---|---|---|
| SALES | x | | x | x | x | x | x |
| MARKDOWNS | | X | x | x | | | x |
| BUYING MARGIN | | | x | x | | | x |
| SALES MARGIN | | | x | x | | | x |
| STOCK FORWARD COVER | x | | x | x | X | x | x |
| STOCK ANNUAL TURN | x | | x | x | x | X | x |
| ROII | x | | x | x | x | x | X |

## Profit

The success of any business is measured by the value of the profit it delivers. In order that this is reached it should be well understood as to what profit is and in what forms it is expressed.

The vital methods to ensure the achievement of profit targets can be broadly defined as

Maximising sales

The careful management of stock commitment to achieve the sales

Through not over buying or under buying

Keeping the level of mark down under control within the set targets

The negotiation of appropriate cost prices

Concentrating on the management of sales margins as profit is made from sales and not intake

Focus on the monetary value as it is that what is banked and not the percentage

The careful management of expenses translates directly into profit.

## Gross profit

is defined as the amount which is available after the direct costs of product at the point of sale are deducted from the value for which they are sold. The outlays comprise of the cost of the product, warehousing, royalties, packaging origination and samples.

*Illustratively the determination of the gross profit can be displayed as follows*

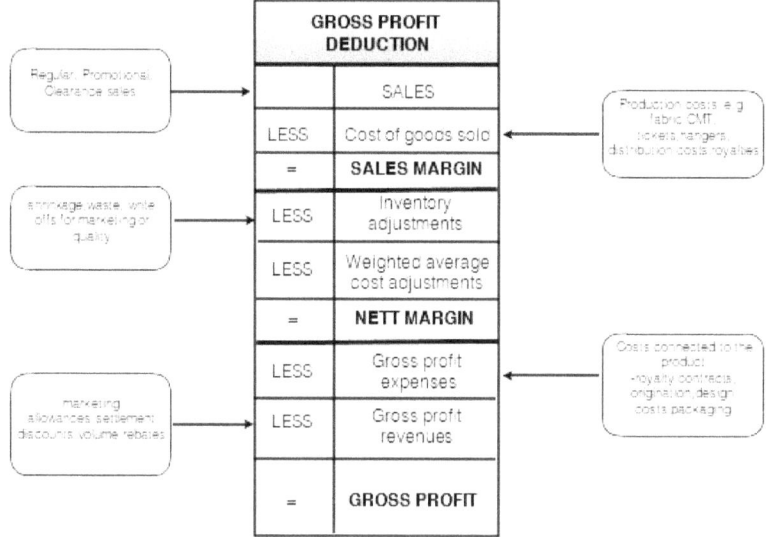

## Profit before tax or net profit

is the amount left over after the gross profit is reduced by the non-direct product overhead costs such as rent, salaries, transport, packing materials, as well as the unpredictable costs like markdowns, quality returns, spoilage and unforeseen costs like unplanned airfreighting. Revenues in the form of volume incentives and settlement discounts from suppliers will in turn improve the net profit.

The expenses of the business that are not directly linked to the product such as salaries, store costs, cost of support areas like information technology and marketing are apportioned in some way or other to the product, probably through the use of turnover contributions.

*Illustratively the determination of the profit before tax can be displayed as follows*

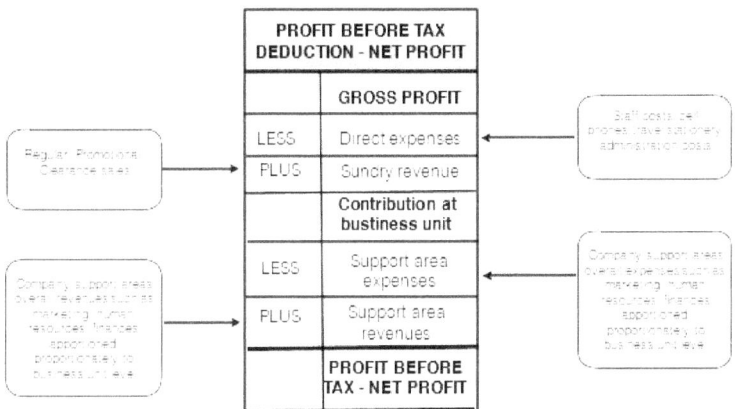

## Profit per square metre

provides an indication of how much profit an item of merchandise delivers from each square metre of space it occupies and consequently the theory is that the allocation of space allocated to a product is dependent on this measurement.

To achieve the highest profit from the available space can be by taking action on low performing items through promotions, reducing the space allotted or replacing the product. The optimum situation is where all products which have the right space allocation will therefore all deliver the same profit per square metre. As the name suggests, the profit per square metre is calculated by dividing the gross profit of an item by the area of selling it occupies.

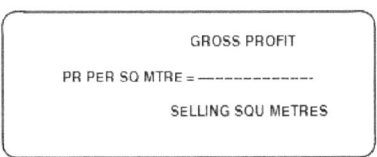

The same principle can be applied by dividing the expenses into the amount of saleable square metreage and therefore the optimum space allocation can also be determined.

Similarly sales per hour and average sales per customer are helpful in terms of staff scheduling and employing staff in functions that are balanced to return an acceptable rate of sale per employee. It should be noted that many or most retailers do not have full time staff members. Therefore to standardise the measurement the number of hours worked is converted to the full time equivalent.

## Return on sales

is the expression of the profit before tax or net profit expressed as a percentage of sales. A deterioration in this measure from one period to another could indicate problems possibly relative to the pricing policy, excessive markdowns or lack of efficient stock control.

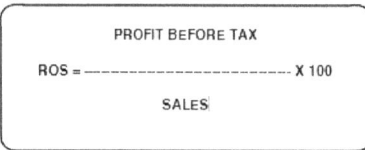

$$ROS = \frac{PROFIT\ BEFORE\ TAX}{SALES} \times 100$$

Assume that the profit before tax is 100,000 and the sales for the same period is 500,000 then the return on sales will be (100,000/500,000) x 100 = 20%

## Break even analysis

reflects how much volume must be sold to cover all costs, both fixed and variable before starting to generate a profit. In other words it is that point where there is no profit or no loss.

# CONCLUSION

There are some significant messages that the reader can be left with after reading through this book. Without doubt, although with the emphasis on planning the financial aspects may look cumbersome and tedious, to some it is nevertheless the foundation of ensuring the maximisation of profits through accurate preparation.

The succesful process of understanding the arithmetic of retail, is underpinned by the common phrase "retail is detail". It is for this reason that a successful and sustainable business is most likely to be achieved if all the the team members develop a deep insight into the mechanisms and formulations that deliver those critical measures. It is without doubt that with such business acumen knowledge there is a better common understanding of the key business objectives and the interaction of all team players is thereby aligned.